Michael Peppiatt

# BACON/ GIACOMETTI

## A DIALOGUE

ERIS *dialogues*

ERIS

An imprint of Urtext
Unit 1 53 Beacon Road
London, SE13 6ED, UK

Copyright © Michael Peppiatt, 2020

Originally published in French as *Giacometti et Bacon: Une rencontre à Londres, 1965* (Paris: L'Echoppe, 2018). Translated by Patrice Cotensin.

Printed and bound in Great Britain

The moral rights of the author and translator have been asserted.

ISBN 978-1-912475-21-6 Paperback
ISBN 978-1-912475-54-4 Hardcover

All rights reserved. No part of this publication may be reproduced, stored in a retrieval system or transmitted in any form or by any means, electronic, mechanical, photocopying, recording or otherwise, without prior permission in writing from Urtext Ltd.

eris.press

## INTRODUCTION

While working on the 'Bacon/Giacometti' exhibition that was shown at the Fondation Beyeler in Basel through the summer of 2018, I did extensive research into the relationship between the two artists, who did not get to know each other well until less than a year before Giacometti's death. As I explored the occasions when the two of them met and spent time together in every available detail, I began to feel I could actually hear them talking...

This 'Dialogue' between Francis Bacon and Alberto Giacometti has in fact been turning slowly in my mind ever since Bacon told me repeatedly about his encounters with Giacometti while the latter was in London to supervise the preparations for his major retrospective at the Tate in 1965. I had met Bacon two years previously to interview him for a student magazine I was editing, and I continued to see him frequently in the years that followed. Bacon had been deeply impressed both by Giacometti's work and by his arduous existence in a tumbledown studio behind Montparnasse which never changed, despite the sculptor's growing fame.

I didn't hear Giacometti's version of their long, animated discussions (one of them lasting through the night), but I had been in thrall to Giacometti both as a man and as an artist ever since Bacon suggested I should go and make myself known to him when I left London to live in Paris. Holding Bacon's letter of introduction in my hand, I paid my first visit to Giacometti's studio in Alésia in January 1966, quite unaware that the sculptor had just died in a hospital near his birthplace in Switzerland. The story might have ended there. The sense that I had missed a unique opportunity, however, made me all the more eager to get to know Giacometti's work and his world intimately. As a result, I met most of his inner circle, from his brother, Diego, and his widow, Annette, to the poets and writers who had been close to him. Once I had read all the interviews he had given and listened to him talking on tape, I could hear and reproduce Giacometti's gravelly voice almost as faithfully as Bacon's more sardonic tones. So, while this 'Dialogue' remains a fiction, it is a fiction deeply rooted in fact.

Michael Peppiatt<br>
August 2020

## BACON/GIACOMETTI: A DIALOGUE

*London, 1965*

*Giacometti is in London to oversee the hang of his big exhibition at the Tate. He has been aware of Bacon and his work for some time, but the two men have grown closer because they have several friends in common, the writer Michel Leiris, the critic David Sylvester and, above all, the artist's model Isabel Rawsthorne, a striking beauty with whom Giacometti had an anguished (and possibly unconsummated) affair. Both artists have made memorable portraits of her.*

*Bacon himself has had a retrospective show at the Tate a couple of years earlier, and since the exhibition travelled to several European museums, he is becoming a name to reckon with both at home and abroad. Still, eight years younger than Giacometti, he is considerably less well-known than the Swiss-born sculptor whose prodigious talents are admired throughout the international art world. Giacometti, however, is already in poor health, and will die the following year.*

*Isabel has organised a couple of dinners in London for Giacometti and Bacon to get to know each other better. Bacon has long admired Giacometti's work, especially his drawings, which he believes are more concentrated and evocative than his sculpture. Struck though he is by the force of Bacon's images, Giacometti remains unconvinced by the English painter's practice of 'attacking' the canvas without any preparatory drawing, since he himself draws constantly every day and makes it the basis of everything he creates.*

*Despite these reservations, the two artists form an immediately cordial rapport. While Giacometti speaks a fluent if strongly accented French, Bacon's grasp of the language is good enough to converse on any subject. Both men love to talk, pulling apart ideas and reconceiving them as they go. This evening they have enjoyed a lavish dinner at Wheeler's fish restaurant, then gone on to the Colony Room, Bacon's favourite drinking club in Soho, to pursue their freely flowing conversation about life, art and their mutual friends. After a while the club starts emptying out, but the two artists, sensing that they may never have another occasion to talk, order more champagne.*

GIACOMETTI Is it true, Francis, that when you raise your glass, you always say 'Champagne for my real friends and real pain for my sham friends'?

BACON That's just an old Edwardian toast people used to use. But since I spend so much of my life drifting from bar to bar and person to person, I do say it from time to time. It seems to sum up the situation so clearly. And after all, Alberto, what else is there to do in life but try to sum the situation up clearly?

GIACOMETTI Yes, of course. That's the only point of anything, and certainly the only point of art, no? I think the aim is to create a kind of residue of reality, not to reproduce reality as such, which is impossible, but to create a reality of equal intensity—its essence, if you like. It's also a way of trying to give existence some form of permanence. Of course you never achieve that. However much you try, you always fail, time after time. And you're bound to fail, because that intensity is always out of your reach. You might think, every now and then, that you've got a little closer, so you keep on trying. And here's the contradiction: nothing would be worse than succeeding, because if you did there'd be nothing left to do!

THEY LAUGH<br>
BACON TOPS UP GIACOMETTI'S GLASS

I love being in London. I don't know why I don't come over more often, and not just to hang a big show like the one at the Tate or to go and look at those fantastic early Egyptian paintings you have at the British Museum. I am in awe of them because they are so lifelike and real. And London is so completely different from Paris. Everything looks different, even the trees in the parks. And the people! They seem to inhabit a different kind of space as they queue so calmly for the bus or make their way along the street. And then these secret little bars and clubs you've taken me to! It's like a different planet.

BACON It's terribly nice of you to say that, Alberto, but I always think Paris is so much more beautiful and stimulating than London. I mean, it often feels terribly provincial and dreary here, and there's really not much happening in the arts. Not much happening in anything, come to that. I remember I always used to long to see the latest issues of *Cahiers d'Art* and those kinds of magazines simply to find out what was happening in Paris. What you were doing, what Picasso was doing...

GIACOMETTI Well, there's your own work, Francis, which I find very exciting and inventive. I went to your gallery yesterday to see the new portraits you've done of your friends, and I have to say that, next to your paintings, which radiate vitality, my things at the Tate will look as though they'd been done by an old spinster!

BACON Alberto, nothing could give me greater pleasure than to hear you—who I consider to be the greatest living artist—say that about my work. I'm hugely, deeply touched. I've admired everything you do and your whole attitude towards life and art from the beginning. It's not just what you've created, but the way you live. I've always been struck by those photos of you in your studio with all its marvellous mess strewn over the floor. I live in that way too, because I find having all that chaos around you stimulates ideas as you work. I've got so many photos and things piled up under foot that I think of it as my 'compost heap', and every time I walk up to the canvas I kick new images up and they act like triggers for ideas while I'm painting. And all the painters I see regularly in London, like Lucian Freud and Frank Auerbach, look up to you as the great figurative artist of our times. You've been a model for us all, particularly now that the art world is only interested in abstract art.

GIACOMETTI Me? A model? I'm no model!

BACON Do you remember, before Isabel introduced us, I saw you sitting at the Flore in Saint-Germain, it must have been in the early fifties, and I felt I had to come over and say that for me you were the greatest living sculptor and draughtsman of our times.

GIACOMETTI And what did I say?

BACON 'What terrible times we must be living in!'

THEY LAUGH
BACON SIGNALS FOR ANOTHER BOTTLE OF KRUG,
WHILE GIACOMETTI LIGHTS YET ANOTHER CIGARETTE

BACON But nobody has managed to convey so much about what it feels like to be a human being now as you have in those marvellous drawings. You manage to sum up so much in a single stroke of the pencil. You even manage to summon up the air, the space and atmosphere surrounding each of the figures you draw, and the figures themselves seem to be spun out of that air. It's magical, especially for me, because I can't draw. I've never been able to. I don't know why, and it's always been one of my limitations. The thing is, I have the image I want to do clearly in my mind, but I don't know how I'm going to achieve it. I go straight to the canvas and hope that as I splash the paint down and move it about it will somehow suggest to me how I can achieve these images that keep dropping into my mind like slides.

GIACOMETTI It must be wonderful to work like that. I'm not really interested in the process of making the actual object. I'd as soon sketch out an idea, then have someone else—an assistant or an artisan—make it into a sculpture. And I'd be delighted if someone else could also do my painting for me. I just want to see this thing that's in my mind actually produced, then perhaps make a few alterations to it here and there. But I couldn't begin to do anything, whether a painting or a sculpture, without drawing it over and over again until I felt I'd more or less got it down.

Ever since I was child, drawing has always been the basis of everything I do. I draw to try to understand what I'm looking at, do you see, to understand the world around me, even though when I'm drawing I often feel like a man groping his way through the dark. For me it's the only way I can grasp what's in front of me, even if it's a glass on a table like this one, or the nose on someone's face. It sounds odd to say that even now I can't really draw a nose, but it's true. When I look at it, when Diego or Annette is sitting there in front of me, their nose just seems to dissolve, or to become so enormous and strange, like a pyramid, that I don't even know where to begin. After all these years, I still can't draw a nose!

BACON Well, it may be that my images are often slapdash—they probably are—even if I do try to make them what's called 'deeply ordered'. I mean, I occasionally do make little sketches in thin paint before I start on a canvas, but they're only the briefest points of departure. I often have the image I want to do very clearly in my mind, but until I begin to work, to get a little paint down and push it around, I've no idea how I'm going to achieve it. That, for me, is the whole mystery of painting and also its tremendous excitement. What I'm always hoping for is to have this great wave of instinct and make these things come off my nervous system as directly and intensely as I can, with all their freshness clinging to them like a foam. It almost never happens like that, of course, but that's another story. I had a dream once— it was ridiculous as most dreams are when you recount them—but I had a fish in my hand, and I thought if only I could slap this fish into the wet plaster on the wall, with all its bones and everything in it, I'd have a perfect painting.

GIACOMETTI For sure.

BACON After all, I only paint for myself, to excite myself by trying to trap these images that sometimes just seem to well up in me one after another.

GIACOMETTI You can only work for yourself. I mean, my only reason for drawing and so on is because I want to understand the world around me a bit better. I have no idea what other people will make of what I've done. I never think about that. I'm sure that the people who look at, or buy, my work are interested in it for completely different reasons than me. For one thing, as far as I'm concerned, no work I've done is ever finished. I always feel it could be improved, or taken further, even if it's already gone into an exhibition or somebody's collection. But for the spectator it's a completely finished work, and of course I can't go around the galleries or people's houses telling everyone the piece is actually still unfinished, can I?

BACON Well, that's the thing, Alberto. When one sees one's things later, one is simply never satisfied with what one's done. Although I believe Henry Moore is.

GIACOMETTI (*laughing*) I saw a huge reclining figure by Moore the other day. It was like the side of a mountain, and I thought I might be able to do some little figures on it, perhaps a little shepherd and a flock of sheep... Then another difference is that I'm just as interested in the failed and destroyed pieces I've made as the ones that go into exhibitions and private collections. Because, in a way, they're all failures. Some perhaps more than others. But it doesn't matter to me, and this is less contradictory than it sounds. I think of failure as inevitable, and if I ever really succeeded, it would be the worst thing in the world. It would be the end—like death, or something even more terrible.

BACON I always aim to make the one great image that will cancel out all the others I've done before. But you're right. If it happened it would be a catastrophe because there would be nothing left to live for. I've always thought that if I didn't have my work, I'd just be a crook or a gambler and drink myself to death. But that single great image won't actually come about, because you can't will these things into being, of course. Particularly in my case, because when I'm painting I leave as much as possible to chance, or what I call 'accident', which is very important to me. And I don't think chance or accident could possibly work for me in the way I hope for if I'd done a whole series of preparatory drawings.

GIACOMETTI Yes, I can see that.

BACON So I just go in like a fool, or a child, in the hope that the first brushstroke will suggest others, and so on, and that all these images that the paint itself seems to indicate will go on indicating or engendering new forms and new possibilities. That's what I love about oil paint, because it's so endlessly fluid and suggestive. And sometimes, when things are going badly, I just put a paint stroke right through the image I'm doing, just like that, to obliterate it. And suddenly, the whole thing comes alive again and I can see how I might make it work.

GIACOMETTI I'd heard about your fascination with 'chance', Francis, and I know you're a great gambler—in life just as in painting! I don't think so much about chance, though of course it's always good to have chance on your side when you're working. What has always intrigued me enormously is how scale changes everything one sees, like the little people walking down the opposite side of the street when you're sitting on one of the café terraces, and how you convey this dramatic difference when you're drawing or painting or modelling your memories of them. I was going to meet Isabel on Boulevard Saint-Michel one night, and I saw her from far off silhouetted against a huge doorway in a dark building. She looked so tiny and so vulnerable. I've never forgotten that vision. And when I tried to recreate it, I could have put her on a huge plinth to suggest the sense of scale, but I wanted to stay close to the first sensation I had. And as I worked to capture it, my sculptures began to diminish in size. They got smaller and smaller, until they crumbled into dust, into nothing.

BACON I've always particularly admired your very small sculptures.

GIACOMETTI In the end, I think, the simplest things can be the most memorable. I mean, this glass in front of me, if you look at it in a certain light, it can be the most compelling sight in the world, as magnificent as some palace in India. I could copy it for the rest of my life without ever really penetrating its mystery. Everything for me has mystery. Sometimes I think I could spend the rest of my life drawing the same chair, over and over, without ever exhausting the subject—or even defining it. And then, if you think of the face of someone who poses for you every day, who you try to capture every day... When you see something new, something unforeseen, appear on that face, it's like the greatest adventure, the greatest discovery, in the world.

BACON Well, you're right, a face can be a simply inexhaustible subject, because it's always changing, always different.

GIACOMETTI You know, once, not long after the war, I was watching the news in a cinema in Montparnasse and all the images on the screen suddenly looked to me like black and white blobs dancing around. I couldn't focus on them and they lost all interest as far as I was concerned. But when I looked at the people sitting in the seats on either side of me, they seemed incredibly fascinating and present, overwhelming even, like huge presences I hadn't properly noticed before. And so did the trees and the streets when I came out of the cinema onto the Boulevard du Montparnasse. Everything looked new, as if I was seeing the world, discovering it, for the first time, as if up until then I'd been looking at it through screens...

BACON You've just said a very profound thing, Alberto. In a way we all live screened existences, and when people complain, as they do, that my paintings are violent, I think it's merely that I've been able to clear a few of those screens away and show life as it is. After all, you can't be more violent than life itself. People complain about cruelty, about bullfights and things as they eat their steaks and lamb cutlets and stand around in fur coats with dead birds in their hair and feathers and things in their hats. It's so mad! After all, we all live off one another. I mean, life itself is so cruel and violent. You only have to open a newspaper to see how cruel everyday life is. All I'm trying to do is to convey a certain reality.

GIACOMETTI  Well, yes. There is violence in everything: in sculpture, in life itself, as you say. When I'm drawing a head, I'm constantly astonished by all the violence it conveys—to live, just to exist, requires such enormous reserves of energy, that the whole thing radiates violence. That's understood, but then, on top of that, you have to ask yourself what that 'reality' you mentioned is. You might say that if I manage to copy this champagne glass in front of me, with its exact shape and the way the light falls on it, that's 'reality'. But even then, you're never actually copying the glass, you're simply copying the residue of its appearance in your eyes as you look at it from every angle, from a distance or from up close. And that itself is always changing, because your point of view never stays the same...

Sometimes I think I live entirely in my own reality, which is quite separate from anybody else's. And I must try to understand it, to get a grip on it—in order to nourish myself, to protect myself, to survive!

BACON Well, *au fond*, this is the thing, Alberto. We do what we do to survive. I wouldn't let out the thoughts and feelings I put into my pictures if I didn't have to live. It's only by painting that my life has any meaning at all. I adore life even if I think of it as meaningless. After all, from birth to death, we simply drift from nothing to nothing, and I think only by our drives, by our passions and appetites, do we give any meaning at all to existence.

GIACOMETTI You talk as if you once believed— perhaps as a child—that life had a meaning and then you were disappointed when you found out that it didn't. I think I've always remained a child. I think I haven't really changed much since I was a boy of about twelve. But somehow I never expected anything. I was too obsessed with trying to understand what I saw immediately around me to search for any other meaning. But now I really hate it when I'm called an Existentialist, as if I belonged to some philosophical school. I don't belong to anything. I barely belong to myself. I'm just trying to understand. No? I mean, people talk about Existentialism as if it's something completely new and people hadn't lived in doubt and anxiety before. It's ridiculous. People have always lived in doubt and anxiety right through history.

BACON You're absolutely right, Alberto. I actually think most real artists, although of course there are very few real artists as you know, stay close to their childhood sensations. And I agree that calling you an Existentialist is ridiculous and totally misses the point. It's the same thing for me, you know. People keep saying that I'm an Expressionist, whatever that means. But I'm not. After all, I've got nothing to express. In fact, I loathe Expressionism with all its ghastly loose puddles of paint! I actually think—if I think about those things at all—that I'm a realist. I'm only trying to make my sensations about life come back to me more strongly and more poignantly.

GIACOMETTI Realism has become a dirty word these days!

BACON In the end, I've been influenced by absolutely everything, because I've looked at everything and it's all gone in and been ground up in my imagination. I mean, I've looked enormously at Egyptian sculpture and things because I think of them as the greatest art man has ever made, but I've also looked at prehistoric art, at the great masterpieces of the Renaissance, at Rembrandt's extraordinary self-portraits, at Manet and Degas, and of course at van Gogh. I've even done a series of Popes after the Velázquez portrait of Pope Innocent X, which I think is perhaps the greatest portrait ever made, even if the things I did to it didn't really work at all and, I have to say, I'm a bit ashamed of them now. But you've looked at the whole history of art, too, Alberto. One senses the presence of the great masters right through your work.

GIACOMETTI Of course! How else could one learn, or have any idea what to do? You have to acquire some sense of the rules, even if you are going to break them...

BACON Above all if you're going to break them...

GIACOMETTI Absolutely. As our writer friend, Michel Leiris, said once, 'if there are no rules, there is no game'. Painting after all is a deeply cultured activity. You have to know what has been done before in order to do anything new. Even as a child, because my father was a painter, I was aware of all kinds of art, and I began copying all kinds of things, from Assyrian and Egyptian art to Giotto and Dürer. I must have copied things in the Louvre 50,000 times. It was like an obsession. And, like you, Francis, I also copied that marvellous portrait by Velázquez, because I agree it's one of the finest portraits in the world. But nowadays the young artists all think that's very passé, that you shouldn't copy at all but be totally original and reinvent everything, like the Surrealists.

BACON Well, people often talk about Surrealism in relation to my work too. I don't like being branded a Surrealist any more than an Expressionist, even though it's true that when I was a very young man I spent quite a bit of time in Paris in the 1920s and Surrealism, which was all the rage then as you know, did open me up to new attitudes and ideas about life as well as art. I think it taught me a lot about the importance of technique, and how technique and subject had to interlock and become completely inseparable. Surrealism probably had all the more effect on me because there was nothing of that kind of intellectual upheaval, with all the challenges to tradition and the desire to renew, happening here in London. For somebody who had seen so little of life, having been brought up on a horse-breeding farm in Ireland, you can imagine what an impact the whole Surrealist thing had on me.

GIACOMETTI Yes, of course.

BACON By the way, how fortunate you are to have people like Michel Leiris and Sartre and Genet writing about your work. We have nobody of that quality writing about art here, I'm afraid. I also think how marvellous it would be to have someone really tearing into your work and telling you what to do, like Pound when he cut and edited the Eliot poem.

GIACOMETTI  Leiris is a very old friend, of course, but he's too modest to make a critique of my work. Perhaps that's why we've stayed good friends! Sartre wouldn't think twice about it, but then I don't think he has much of an eye. However clever he is with ideas, with concepts, he can't actually see a painting. Genet, on the other hand, has a real sense of what I'm trying to do, and I think his book about my studio is unusually perceptive. Anyway, the Surrealists certainly dominated the early part of my life in Paris. I got caught up with them in the late 1920s and, like you, I'd come from a very different background. Imagine going straight from an isolated village in the Swiss mountains to the inner circles of Montparnasse in its heyday! Most of the Surrealists were about my age and very bright and charming, full of crazy ideas about how everything could be changed and reinvented. And I liked a lot of them personally, not just the painters like Ernst and Miró, but the writers as well: Éluard, Crevel, even Breton for a time (I was actually best man at his wedding, you know). And through them I got to know a whole side of Paris—collectors, decorators, dealers, society people—that I probably wouldn't have come across otherwise. That helped me a great deal, because one of the decorators, Jean-Michel Frank, asked me to do decorative objects for his clients, which meant that my brother Diego and I managed to earn some money to pay our way...

BACON Oh, I didn't know you'd worked for a decorator—and what's more by far the best decorator in Paris. That's very curious, because when I started out I did something similar, not for somebody as accomplished as Frank of course... But I did design some carpets and chairs and things, but they were all very derivative and now I wish I hadn't done anything of the kind. I'm sure your decorative things were much better. Still, as you say, they did help one to keep going at the time.

GIACOMETTI So, since I was in contact with the Surrealists the whole time, I absorbed a lot of their ideas, and I started doing a completely new kind of sculpture, full of wild fantasies and sly references. I was showing off, proving that I could do things that were just as weird and perhaps even weirder than any that the others had done. And this went on for several years until I eventually realised I'd been on the wrong path and none of it was making any sense. It was no more than masturbation, and I needed to get back to working from life, from a model.

Of course, Breton didn't like that at all—'anybody can draw a head', he said—and one day he and some of the others lured me into a meeting and formally kicked me out of the movement. The Pope of Surrealism excommunicated me! I also lost quite a few good friends when I left, which I regretted, but, in a sense, it was the best thing that could have happened to me.

BACON Well, it must have been marvellous to have known all those people and gone around with them. For some reason I hardly ever seem to meet people I can really talk to. I suppose it's partly because I find so many of what's called 'intellectuals' so boring, and then with my sort of gilded gutter life, going from bar to bar, person to person, I rarely meet really intelligent people. I meet drunks mostly, and people who are in despair. I'd love to meet someone who dominated me, both mentally and physically, a sort of Nietzsche of the football team, but I'm afraid to say that's very rare. Now, I'm not saying that my new friend, George, is the Nietzsche of the football team but he does have the kind of physique, the kind of muscular, male voluptuousness that I love to paint.

GIACOMETTI Ah, I liked George very much, even though I'm afraid we couldn't communicate very much when you brought him to dinner the other evening.

BACON I'm so glad you liked him, Alberto. I've become very fond of him. I only wish he'd learn something, because as you know he used to earn his living by breaking into people's houses and things and stealing but, unfortunately, he was always getting caught, so he's spent a good bit of time in prison. The thing is, as an East Ender, he was born into stealing, it was like a tradition, because it's what his whole family did. I'm trying to take him out of that life because the next time he's caught he'll get a really long stretch in jail. Since George is very good with his hands, I've tried to get him to learn a trade like gilding, which I believe earns quite good money. But, naturally, he prefers going out and getting dead drunk instead. That sounds a bit mad coming from an old drunk like me, but even when I've been on the drink for days I always know I have to work—even with a bad hangover, which sometimes actually makes my mind crackle with electricity and helps me to concentrate. But now that I give him money George doesn't know what to do with himself. I even tried to get him to learn French, but of course that was a total washout.

GIACOMETTI Send him to me in Paris, Francis. I will get him speaking French, and my brother, Diego, will find him some work to do, perhaps making stands for sculpture. It would be a pleasure to help George. Perhaps

I have fallen for him, like you, Francis. Do you know, when I'm in London, I always feel homosexual! You must take me some time to what you call your queer clubs. I'd like to see what goes on there. I love places where people go for sex because they have a special atmosphere. We had the famous 'Sphinx' club in Paris, where I often went at the end of the evening because I knew quite a few of the girls there, and I could simply sit there and watch them, which I loved, and make drawings of them because they had this extraordinary presence as they stood around there, like these incredible goddesses. They were perfectly happy if you bought them a few drinks. Even if you wanted something more than that, you just paid them what they asked for and they didn't care whether you managed to do it or not. And that was the end of it. They didn't start clinging to you, as women often do afterwards.

My life with Annette has become much easier, much freer, now that she has an apartment of her own and lovers of her own. I think I told you about this girlfriend I have, called Caroline, who comes to my studio to sit for me regularly, and she is a marvellous model for me. Annette knows about her, and she's not at all pleased I'm afraid, even though I actually encourage her to have her own lovers. So I do what I can to make sure the two of them never come into contact. But last night Caroline just turned up out of the blue at the little hotel Annette and I are staying at near Victoria Station. She's gone away again now, as quickly as she came, and I don't even know why she made the trip. She's just like that. She comes and she goes and you don't know why.

BACON Lovers do get very possessive. I used to know a man called Peter Lacy—I painted him a great deal at one point—who'd had his nerves shattered from being a Spitfire pilot during the war. And he used to make the most impossible scenes, beating me up and destroying my work. He'd go mad at times and go round breaking all the furniture. We were on a long boat trip once and he thought I was making eyes at all the stewards, who are always queer of course on those kinds of luxury boats. So Peter got into a rage and pushed all my clothes out through the porthole and I had nothing left, not even a pair of shorts, to wear! But there it was. I'd become obsessed with him. It was like that song: I couldn't live with him, and I couldn't live without him. We had these three years of absolute hell together. And then when that exhibition of mine opened at the Tate, among the telegrams that came to congratulate me I got this one saying he had just died in Tangiers. But it was a kind of suicide. He set out to do it by drinking so many bottles of whisky a day that his pancreas simply exploded.

GIACOMETTI It's true that falling in love can get you into terrible situations. Caroline has all these connections with the underworld in Paris, and some of the people she deals with are real gangsters. I was in a bar with a young poet friend not long ago when these men Caroline knows came in with guns and everybody in the place ducked under the tables, and then they shot all the bottles and mirrors in the bar to pieces. I think they were giving someone a warning. It was very impressive! Anyway, I always give her 'protectors', or whatever they are, all the money they ask for and then they leave us alone, at least for a while.

You know, I was really happy to see Isabel again at dinner this evening, Francis. She still fascinates me and I've never met any other woman like her, she's a wonderful friend and we just seemed to pick up at the point where we'd left off the last time we met at the Coupole in Paris. She was also a wonderful model for me, even though I felt quite intimidated by her reputation as a maneater, which I know has been well-earned!

BACON Well, a woman-eater as well, if her affair with Balthus's wife is anything to go by. Isabel just has this extraordinary vitality, she's sort of omnivorous, whether it's for people, or drink, or God knows what else. People tend to think of women as dainty, you know, but Isabel is tougher than most men I've known.

But then of course, once you get to know them, most men are weak, unfortunately.

GIACOMETTI We are all weak, Francis. Man is a kind of aberration, especially if you compare him to something like the trees that are all around us. Recently I've been drawing trees for a book about Paris, a book called *Paris Without End* that Tériade wants to publish, and I'm struck by how self-contained and majestic they are. I only need to see one tree, that's quite enough. Already two trees are too much, so now I would never take a walk in the forest because it would be too much, too overwhelming. Just as I wouldn't want to see more than one glass. One glass already poses too many problems. What is comforting, anyway, is that trees don't need any answers because they have no questions about their existence. They simply are. We'd all be better off as trees, really.

BACON Well, I'm not sure I'd actually want to be a tree. Whenever I'm surrounded by trees and what's called 'nature', with all those things singing outside your window in the morning, I can't stand it. I just long to get back to a city with streets and people. Just to walk along streets and see people going about their daily round. I loathe the countryside.

GIACOMETTI (*laughing*) I understand. And I've noticed that most of your paintings and portraits are inside four walls. But so are mine, it's true, and even if I do draw or paint the occasional landscape, I am only really at home in cities too. I used to walk round Paris late at night with Sam Beckett, usually after we'd drunk a few whiskies in bars like Chez Adrien or the Rosebud, and we were going down past the Montparnasse cemetery once and he suddenly cried out: 'I can't look at trees any longer.' And I said to him: 'That's because you love them so much, Sam.'

BACON I often wonder about Beckett, Alberto. I mean, I know he's meant to be so profound about man's condition and so on, but I've never really seen the point of all those tramps sitting about in dustbins on the stage, talking endlessly. I've known plenty of those down-and-outs around the bars and places in Soho, so I don't actually need to go and see them in the theatre.

GIACOMETTI I did a very bare, plaster tree for a production of Beckett's *Waiting for Godot* at the Odéon a few years ago. I don't think it worked. I don't think Beckett thought it really worked either. But like me he accepts failure, he accepts that everything we do, however hard we work at it, is bound to fail. 'Fail again', he says somewhere, 'Fail better.' I think that's where he's clear-sighted and profound. And I don't know how it sounds in English, but in French he writes so well.

BACON Well, of course, we do fail. We always fall short. What makes me come back to the canvas time and again, even though I feel I've done nothing but one failure after another, is the idea that I might do the one perfect image that cancels all the others out. I have this absurd optimism that one day I will achieve that, even though I know it's an impossibility to do.

GIACOMETTI I think you have come very close, Francis. Some of your new portraits—those of George, for instance—that I saw yesterday are stronger than anything I have seen in years. They carry a freshness and vigour that no one else in our time has achieved, and somehow by constructing those kinds of cages round your figures you make them doubly vivid and powerful. You are the greatest living artist.

BACON (*with tears starting in his eyes*) You can't say that, Alberto. Of course, I'm hugely, deeply, touched. But it's you whom I've admired, who's been like a god to me over the years, not only in your absolute search for the truth and the whole vision you've created but for the way you've lived, completely dedicated to what you do whatever happens. It's no surprise that those cages you mention come from you. I know that, even though I've looked at everything and everything has had its influence on me. I've always found the cage terribly useful as a space frame for concentrating attention on the central image. It also helps create perspective, which has always been a problem for me when I'm organising the space in my pictures. But this only goes to show... It's you who's by far and away the greatest living artist. I don't even compare.

GIACOMETTI No. I have to say it once more. I want to be quite clear. It's you, Francis, who's the greatest living artist.

BACON Alberto, it's always been you. You are...

> THEY ARE BOTH BEGINNING TO LAUGH NOW
> BACON SHAKES THE LAST DROPS FROM THE
> CHAMPAGNE BOTTLE INTO THEIR GLASSES
> THEY RISE UNSTEADILY, AND CLINK

GIACOMETTI What was it, Francis? 'Champagne for my real friends...'

> THEY FALL INTO EACH OTHER'S ARMS

Michael Peppiatt left London in 1966 for a job as arts editor at *Réalités* and then *Le Monde* in Paris, where he lived at the heart of the art and literary world for the following thirty years. In 1985 he bought *Art International*, relaunching the magazine from his apartment in Paris. Peppiatt is the author of a dozen books, including *Francis Bacon: Anatomy of an Enigma*, *In Giacometti's Studio*, *Interviews With Artists*, and the acclaimed memoirs, *Francis Bacon in Your Blood* and *The Existential Englishman*.